Feathered Dreams

FEATHERED DREAMS

celebrating birds
in poems, stories & images

JANET M. RUTH

Mercury HeartLink
www.heartlink.com

In Memory

of my parents, Marge and Paul Ruth,
who first instilled in me
a love of birds and the outdoors,
inspiring both a scientific research career
and the poems and stories in this book

FEATHERED DREAMS

HERE

THERE

EVERYWHERE

Preface

The contents of *Feathered Dreams*—my love song to birds—comprise the images and words that need saying but did not fit into my scientific journal articles.

This book is dedicated to everyone who loves birds. I want to especially honor those who labor daily to conserve birds and the habitats they rely on around the world, so that our nieces and nephews, our grandchildren, can still celebrate winged multitudes. During my scientific research career, I had the privilege to work with Partners in Flight (PIF)—a coalition of federal and state agencies, conservation organizations, industry, and academia—to promote landbird conservation in the Western Hemisphere [http://www.partnersinflight.org]. PIF has joined a global effort by National Geographic, Cornell Lab of Ornithology, National Audubon Society, and BirdLife International, along with many other groups, to designate 2018 *The Year of the Bird*. They are celebrating the centennial anniversary of the U.S. Migratory Bird Treaty Act, the most powerful bird-protection law passed by Congress, in conjunction with the international Migratory Bird Treaty. The aim of these efforts is to "heighten public awareness of birds because of their wonder and beauty—and because they symbolize nature's interconnectedness and the importance of caring for our shared planet."

This book of bird poems, stories, artwork, and photographs, fledged during *The Year of the Bird*, conveys how birds capture my imagination, and how they connect us with Nature. For without our Mother, we are lost. In words, lines, and shadows we see birds here, and there, and everywhere. Feathers, wings, and spirits populate our days and nights, our waking and dreaming. I hope to inspire love and conservation of birds as well as the habitats that they, and we, require to live happily and peacefully on this planet.

HERE

The poet's eye, in a fine frenzy rolling,
doth glance from heaven to earth,
from earth to heaven;
and as imagination bodies forth
the forms of things unknown,
the poet's pen turns them to shape,
and gives to airy nothing
a local habitation and a name.

—William Shakespeare, *A Midsummer Night's Dream*

Swift Angels

Mom was the unstated backbone of the family.

> *I meant to write about the bobolink,*
> *but chimney swifts hijacked my thoughts.*

Unlike Dad, a Gilgamesh-type,
Mom never thought of herself as the heroine
of her own story, let alone anyone else's.

> *No elaborate plumage,*
> *just a sooty brown to match roosting sites that*
> *gave them their name.*

Yet as a young woman from a Nebraska farm
in the 1950s, she accepted a call
to give her secretarial skills to the church,
first half-way across the country in Pennsylvania,
then half-way across the world in Europe, where
Dorothy Gale met Gilgamesh.

> *They chirp and twitter madly overhead,*
> *little feathered cigars with wings.*

As a child, I heard her rise before winter dawn,
tiptoe downstairs to turn up the thermostat,
then the "ping-pong-ball-bouncing" sound as
heated water rose into the radiator in my room.

Twisting and turning through the heavens,
aerial acrobats capture insects to feed chicks
in nests plastered to the inside of chimneys.

A mean word never passed her lips.
Mom lived a frugal life—recycled plastic bags,
sewed her own clothes. She taught me to sew,
no easy task since I did not inherit her patience.
After retiring she learned to quilt and blessed us all.

Avian scythes slice the sky above my head
into twisting ribbons of cerulean.

A slip of a woman under the best of circumstances,
the surgery and the cancer reduced her to a
featherweight of her former self.

From high in the sky
a coffee-colored feather
drifts on the wind,
floats into my trembling hand.

I sit at her bedside with my brothers and sister,
stand watch beside her. The well-loved life force
contracts within her body's barely recognizable shell,
concentrates for one last brave act.

The evening is drawing close like a blanket.
I look up into the heavens—
filled with a host of circling, fluttering swifts.

Then the labored breathing ceases.
There is silence.
This tiny, unassuming woman—
> iron bond with our past,
> gentle arms that cradled us all,
> who sent us into the world
> on our own adventures—
has escaped.
She marshalled the strength for one final leap
into what was, for her, not unknown.

I don't know how to balance
celebration of her life
with the grieving.

> *The setting sun illuminates*
> *their brown-feathered heads,*
> *transformed with golden halos.*

Winter Secrets

Air is knife-sharp this morning in the cold.
Midnight flaps overhead: crows from their roost.
All wait for sun to open eye of gold
onto shortened winter days. Light is loosed,
illuminates white cottonwood fingers
that lift budding ruby candles aloft.
Piñon smoke's bitter blue-gray taste lingers,
drifts. Acequia dust sifts, trodden soft.
Across my path a streak of feathers slinks.
Halts. Roadrunner—head and tail form a "V"—
stealthy stalker rattles his beak and blinks.
Cuidado! quail whisper from sagebrush sea.
Be alert and look. Life signs are covert
in wind and sand of a winter desert.

In the Vineyard

Midnight
new moon
the barn owl
scrapes talons
across the
chalkboard
of her screech
sails on
silent wings
seeks warm sip
voluptuous burgundy
bouquet of iron
crunchy bolus
of splintered
bones.

Pupils dilated
deer mouse
crouches
shrinks
in the dark.
Rising acrid
astringent
fear rasps
tiny throat.

Viscous
insidious brew
simmers metallic
in murine belly
leaves
coppery finish
on its tongue
in the moment
just before. . .

ACTS OF SPRING

Sky above the Río Grande,
above the Sandias,
stretches pale cerulean,
thin mares' tail clouds
gallop in from the west—
omens of change.
Cochiti Dam has paroled
imprisoned water
to make room for snowmelt.
The river runs bank-full.
Cottonwood and New Mexico olive leaves
clothe winter's bony fingers
in lacy green gloves.

Beneath this arc of change,
I stand among last year's rustling
dead leaves and fallen twigs,
strain to hear a whisper,
to see a sign.

Bubbling from the silence,
a saucy whistle, syncopation,
clattering *CHACK! CHACK!*
from a feathered sprite.
I twist and pry, peer and peek
through foliage—
nothing.

Completely still,
the chatter mocks me.
My eyes *in a fine frenzy rolling*,*
ready to give up,
I am at last rewarded with a glimpse—
Puck, in yellow and white robes,
launches on olive wings
into the heavens with a wink,
then plummets free,
back into the thicket—

yellow-breasted chat has returned.

* *A Midsummer Night's Dream,* Act 5, Scene 1

EMERGENCE

The meadowlark explodes into flight
from the nest, camouflaged in golden bunchgrass
at my feet.
My thrumming heartbeats slow,
stooping, I part bristly curtain—
a roof, a tunnel
       woven of last year's dry stems frames
          vault entrance, protecting

two wobbly heads, scrawny necks,
bits of damp gray down cling to diminutive pink bodies,
       trembling. Nestlings can barely move their heads,
blue-black eyelids sealed tight against the world, bruised
by escape from snug, ovoid universe
       into frightening expanse.
Frail bodies rest against
one white and brown-blotched microcosm,
still intact.

Lifting this unpretentious egg that rivals Fabergé,
I discover it is not intact,
a minute chip, a hair-line crack mars
smooth porcelain surface—

      the egg is pipping!

Inside, a chick struggles to climb up
      through the *sipápu* in the shell of its first world,
        to emerge into the second.

Holding this capsule of life to my cheek,
I feel tapping. . . . Using the egg tooth
on its beak, a fragile chick
chisels through walls of the only universe it knows,
sends messages in fierce meadowlark Morse code.

Cradling this ferocious creature, I wonder—
do we have the meadowlark's animal courage,
instinct for transformation,
would we take a hammer to the cracked facades
of the only world we know?

FEATHER MITES I

whirring wings
in arcs of sound
black-chinned hummingbird
listening female perched
hearts pounding

red-shafted swag across winter sky
flicker shrieks *KEER — CHEER*

grasshopper sparrow
my palm kissed with feathers
a fleeting joy

ominous rumble
stygian clouds lanced
by lightning
raven plummets
from the rift

new year
an uplifting twitter
from winter junco

bill clacker
tail pumper
lizard snapper
roadrunner—
neovelociraptor

Summer Morning

Pond water
splatters onto backs of gold-and-black speckled koi
suspended above murky bottom.

Delicate vanilla and chai aromas
waft from fragile porcelain cup
adorned in purple pansies and creamy violets,
rim gleams gold—a gift from mother.
Diaphanous breeze
tickles cottonwood leaves,
casts a mosaic of light and plum shadows
onto the patio,
riffles the golden-brown surfaces of
tea and pond.

A diminutive feather dances at my feet.
I pick it up,
examine perfect meshed,
pearl-gray barbules at blunt tip,
airy silver down at base,
all attached to rachis—
sooty center line.

Releasing the dreamy wisp,
I watch it float away, skitter on a breeze,
free of purpose—

formerly lining the breast of what bird?
　　　perhaps curve-billed thrasher screaming
　　　　　wheet WHEET from the roof looks for it,
　　　or mourning dove *coo*-ing at her nest
　　　　　with two porcelain eggs in the cliffrose,
　　　or Gambel's quail giving squeaky hinge
　　　　　alarm calls, crying *cuidado* in the sand sage.
　　　Rufous hummingbird shatters my reverie
　　　　　with his harsh *ZEE-chuppity-chup*,
　　　　　banishes all others from the feeder.

The feather is not his—
　　　small,
　　　　　but not small enough.

ৎ　　ৎ　　ৎ　　ৎ　　ৎ

My mind drifts
on this morning when I need do nothing.
My gaze flits lightly across
　　　chocolate flowers tumbling onto patio,
　　　　　spreading cocoa scent on the breeze,
　　　scarlet geraniums suspended above me,
　　　burgeoning basil destined for pesto,
　　　crispy, dry remains of tomato plant,
　　　　　denuded by an army of hornworms
　　　　　that I find difficult to hate—too much—
　　　those that escape our vigilant plucking

morph into pink-and-brown hawk moths,
hover and probe evening flowers
like wee six-legged hummingbirds.

Honk from burro down the street,
and last-ditch crow
from our neighbor's handsome Polish rooster,
portend the sun climbing above cottonwood shade,
dragging with it a blanket of midday summer heat.
I gather pen, paper,
        empty cup, thoughts,
           retreat inside.
Swamp cooler rattles and hums awake,
      to strive valiantly against the swelter
         and what passes for humidity
         in the New Mexico desert.

GOLD

—after Walter de la Mare's poem "Silver"

Hot and shimmering, now the sun
Paces the day at a golden run;
To the west, below, he peers, and spies
Golden lizards with golden eyes;
All day long the adobes hold
His rays, his heat, his fire of gold;
Crouched in the shade with a golden coat
And amber eyes naps the coyote;
From shadowy sagebrush, quail chicks peep
'Neath their mother in golden-feathered sleep;
The antelope-squirrel will barely stir,
With golden claws and golden fur;
Wriggling tadpoles, an orgy foretold—
The bleating cacophony of spadefoot toad;
And golden butterflies float so fair
With gossamer wings on golden air.
Beneath the heat of the golden sun,
We swelter and pine for the silver moon.

HELD HOSTAGE BY "TRASHERS"

Once again, I unhook the screen door, stealthily pick my way between flowering spikes of red yucca and trumpet-shaped sacred datura flowers. In the cool summer morning, daturas are luminous with absorbed moonlight. As the sun climbs higher, they will close like twisted rags, redirect their energy to form prickly seedpods that hang like thorny lanterns beneath the leaves.

!@#! *Ouch!*—too close to a rosebush and my calf sports a long red scratch. Sometimes even I am amazed at the lengths to which we go to minimize disturbance to the pair of curve-billed thrashers nesting in the cholla by our front sidewalk. We are reduced to creeping through the bushes to get to the gate. Alternate escape routes are currently blocked by nesting mourning doves. In a panic, doves blast off from one nest on an abandoned garbage can whenever the electronic garage door opens, or one in the trumpet vine by the back gate when we empty scraps into the compost bin. The commotion threatens to bounce their eggs from the poorly tossed-together twigs that pass for a nest. But the stars of this story are the thrashers, much more intrepid nest protectors.

Birders have the strange, endearing habit of giving birds nicknames that approximate their real names. Tanagers become "teenagers," quail become "Quaaludes," and—my favorite—a caracara becomes a "face-face" (the Spanish word for face is *cara*). But perhaps most accurate are the "trashers." Curve-billed thrashers are well-known denizens of southwestern arid shrublands. With their insistent, loud *wheet WHEET*s, they are one of my favorite backyard birds in the desert near Albuquerque. Ground foragers, thrashers probe with long, decurved bills for insects or seeds. Our sidewalk and patio are littered with bark mulch, twigs and sand that foraging thrashers have tossed aside. Periodically I rescue a plant whose base has been completely exposed by these diligent mulch-tossers. Nothing consoles my husband as he grumbles and sweeps the sidewalk—again.

Chapter One—the story had begun in April. A thrasher pair messed around in the cholla, fiddling with twigs from the previous year's nest, then began construction on a new nest next door. I assumed this was the same pair as in the previous year. Pairs are known to maintain permanent territories from one year to the next and often locate nests only 30-100 meters from the previous year's nest. Our cholla contains the ragged remnants of several former thrasher abodes. They constructed the base of the nest from dry twigs arranged in a loose but stable configuration fortified by the cholla branches. Both male and female worked on the nest.

Just as in the previous year, after having partially constructed a nest, "our" thrashers disappeared. Was the neighborhood not to their liking? I don't know. But they return in mid-May to pick up construction where they'd left off. This pair appears to have several favorite nest spots within their territory, which can be two to four hectares. My hypothesis—they build several partial or trial nests and then decide which one to use first. Usually our pair's first nest is in an as-yet-undiscovered location. Then, after they fledge a first brood or the nest has failed, they return to the partial nest in our cholla for their second brood.

One thrasher clambers around in the "nest," poking, probing, and shifting twigs, while the other perches nearby watching the proceedings. They make little pair-bonding noises—purring, muttering, puttering murmurs—the thrasher equivalent of whispered sweet nothings. After the main nest framework is in place, they line it with fine grasses. One of the adults takes advantage of a failed gardening experiment—a grass plant that I had dug up and potted in hopes of eventual transplanting. It reaches up, grasps a thin strand of dead grass, and pulls sharply until it comes loose.

As it becomes obvious that the thrashers are serious this time, I begin recording more deliberate notes. As an avian biologist and bird-watcher, I find myself equally drawn to the scientifically pertinent facts and the stories that result from hanging out with feathered neighbors. Peering surreptitiously into their lives, I feel a bit like an ornithological voyeur.

26 May: one blue-green egg in the nest! no obvious reddish-brown speckles as described in field guide

28 May: three eggs

29 May: four eggs

Curve-billed thrashers lay a single egg per day, usually for a total of two to four eggs. After the previous year (three eggs), I assume that our thrashers have certainly concluded the clutch with four and begun incubating, which doesn't happen until the female is done laying eggs.

2 June: five eggs!

Revision in notes required—the fifth egg would have been laid on 30 May, with the first full day of incubation on 31 May (Incubation Day 1).

Chapter Two—incubation stage—subsequent observations support my theory that this is the second brood of the year. I watch one adult accompanied by two obvious juveniles—shorter, less-decurved bills, darker streaking on the breast, and dark eyes. They follow the adult around, begging and waiting to have food stuffed down their throats. They are quickly nicknamed "widgets" for the insistent call they make while demanding attention. They appear quite naive about what constitutes food, picking at everything. One adult incubates the second clutch of eggs, while the other chaperones the juvenile delinquents around trying to impress on their little "widget" brains important things like: "This is food, this is not. That is a predator. Here is the seed block that the mammalian bipeds left out in the back yard to pay us for trashing their garden!"

10 June (Incubation Day 11): still five eggs; adults take turns incubating; loud chattering between parents with exchange of nest duties

Our thrashers are tenacious. Once one settles into the nest, all that is visible is a tail sticking straight up, a

decurved bill, and a baleful yellow eye glaring back at me. The thrasher sits tightly on the nest even when we pass within a meter, unlike the fickle mourning doves. I like to think they have come to recognize that we mean them no harm. Perhaps it comes from watching the ridiculous manner in which we try to avoid disturbing them. Then again, they seem to have figured out my strategy for sneaking a peek at the nest: I peer through the screen door for the telltale silhouette of tail and bill. When it's missing, I quickly unhook the screen and scurry over for a peek, stand on tiptoe to see over the rim of the nest, try not to put my eye out on a cholla spine. Frequently a thrasher materializes magically from the sand sage, swoops into the cholla, and scoots onto the nest before I have a chance to see anything. It has become a game with us, perhaps more so for me than the thrashers. They never give alarm calls, but silently foil my plans with a fierce yellow stare.

12 June (Incubation Day 13): three "just-hatched" chicks and two eggs! incubation to hatching—13 days

Chapter Three—nestling stage—first indication of the new development on this day is during parental nest exchange. The incoming bird is carrying food! It perches on the nest, making gentle churring, muttering calls, and does not immediately settle onto the nest. Instead there is activity that I can't see, and the thrasher flies away carrying what could be a fecal sac or egg shell! I hurry out for a peek. In their prickly nursery, the hatchlings are naked, with the exception of a little spiky fuzz, and their bulbous heads are too heavy to lift on their scrawny necks. They lie motionless and I cross my fingers, hoping that they are okay. An adult returns, dives directly into the cholla, and perches anxiously on a nearby branch. As soon as I step back, she slips onto the nest.

13 June (Nestling Day 1): four chicks; one unhatched egg

15 June (Nestling Day 3): four nestlings; one unhatched egg; tips of pin feathers visible on stubby wings, feathers inside pins not yet broken out of sheaths.

By mid-June we are well into summer and afternoon temperatures are in the mid-90's, although it can be chilly at night. The thrashers have a job keeping their nestlings cool. When it gets really hot, the brooding adult straddles the nest with its wings slightly spread to provide shade. I suppose it is too hot to actually sit on the young. The parent opens its beak and pants.

16 June (Nestling Day 4): four nestlings; unhatched egg gone; bright yellow rictal flanges obvious

Rictal flanges are the fleshy, often brightly colored rims around the outside of nestlings' bills. When thrasher nestlings gape, begging to be fed, the flanges provide round yellow targets, showing parents where to stuff the tasty tidbits.

On one occasion during the nestling period, a juvenile from the first brood hangs around "widgeting," peering into the cholla, and picking at bits of bark on the ground. The adult on the nest ignores this behavior, perhaps hoping that the delinquent will go away and stop drawing attention to the nest.

Indeed, the desert is not a safe place for little thrashers. By placing their nest in a spiny fortress, the parents dare all predators (and curious mammalian bipeds) to approach. Undeterred by the formidable thorns, prospective villains keep trying. Occasionally I hear a rapid *snap-snap-snap* and see a greater roadrunner peering curiously into the cholla, snapping its bill. A deep croak alerts me to a hungry common raven. On these occasions I must admit to interfering with "the way of things." I won't be around all the time and then it will be up to the thrashers. The adults don't mob or otherwise aggressively respond to interlopers, but they do scrunch down over the nestlings so as to practically disappear.

The predators' threats to nestling survival were brought home in graphic detail one previous year when thrashers nested in the same cholla. After watching the entire nesting drama and tip-toeing around three large "widgets" teetering on the brink of fledging, Nature, red in tooth and claw, made her presence known. In my study with the window open, I heard a terrible commotion, accented with parental shrieks and nestling cries. I ran out in time to see the carnage but not the guilty party.

The cooing and bill-snapping outside the wall was all the information I needed—the roadrunner had struck. Thrasher parents screamed and flew around in a panic. One nestling had become an unwilling fledgling, hopping around desperately on the ground below the cholla. Another was already dead, crucified improbably on a thorny branch. The third had tumbled from the nest and was impaled on its back in the cholla where it screeched and struggled to free itself. I climbed onto the wall and managed to release it while collecting a shoulderful of cholla spines. The rescued youngster appeared very much alive, placed in the protected patio with its sibling. Unfortunately, it was dead the following day. Apparently its injuries were worse than what I could see. So, one out of three robust nestlings actually made it to "widget-hood" in that round. Life is tenuous for thrashers.

19 June (Nestling Day 7): only three nestlings; no sign of the fourth; no evidence of violence

Food limitations likely determine whether all nestlings are fed and survive to fledge. Although this pair started out with five eggs and then four hatchlings, perhaps the prey base was only sufficient to support three. Our thrasher parents spend more and more time foraging for food to feed the growing nestlings. The chick that hatched last was probably smaller and weaker and couldn't compete with its nest-mates. Adults provide food to the most aggressive chicks and the fourth probably starved. This may seem appalling, but it ensures that the strongest offspring survive. Production of four weaker fledglings could mean the loss of the entire brood.

21 June (Nestling Day 9): three nestlings; fairly large; eyes open; panting

23 June (Nestling Day 11): three nestlings; goofy appearance; heads with tufts of down; pin feathers on

wings and tail extending; feathers beginning to emerge from pins

26 June (Nestling Day 14): three nestlings; ready to fledge; alert; skittish

The nestlings are now almost fledglings. They occasionally sit "next door" in the old nest. Little fluff remains on their plumage. I am particularly careful when I go outside for fear of causing them to fledge prematurely. They clamber back and forth clumsily between the two nests. Noisy, they produce single chip notes and, for the first time, give the "widget" call.

27 June (Nestling Day 15): fledging!

Chapter Four—fledgling stage—one nestling is now officially a fledgling! It hops on the ground near the cholla. Spying me, it panics and heads for the safety of the nest, clambering up through the prickly branches while both parents hover nearby giving alarm calls. I can see another nestling, still in the nest. Fifteen days from hatching to fledging.

By the next day, all three have fledged. They regularly climb back into the cholla when threatened and monotonously issue "widget" calls to anyone who will listen. Within another day, they are gone from the nest vicinity. For several days we hear fledgling chip notes and see "widgets" around the house. They never returned to the nest cholla after that.

30 June: two fledglings follow one adult

Two young thrashers trail after an adult. They watch intently when the parent finds an anthill, grabs individual ants, and feeds them. They observe while bark is flung about in the search for hapless insects. They do no foraging themselves beyond half-hearted pecking at objects of no nutritional value. One picks up a large piece of bark and carries it around proudly for a moment before discarding it; learning to forage for food is a trial-and-error affair. The parents discover suet in the basket feeder which we almost threw away because it had turned into a greasy, drippy mess in the 100-degree heat. An additional protein source! They land on the hanging basket, swing back and forth, reach through the wire, rip off a chunk, and fly away with the loot.

The "widgets" are comical. They hop along the ground, trip over something, take fright at inanimate objects, and flutter off the ground momentarily. They thrash about in shrubs and flap their wings to keep their balance on a branch. I haven't seen more than two fledglings at any one time and fear that one has succumbed to the threats of the big wide world.

> 4 July: hear "widgets" in the saltbush; see adult followed by three fledglings fly over the house

Today is noteworthy for reasons other than the holiday, but equally worthy of fireworks. All three fledglings have survived after all. Later, opening the front screen door, I revel in the fact that we no longer have to sneak through the bushes. I can deadhead the roses, tend to flowers growing below the nest, and remove the drooping dead branch on the cholla.

I am pulled up short. There is a thrasher in the cholla! She appears to be cleaning out the nest. Settling into the nest cup, she gives a little wiggle or two to make sure that it still fits; then she stays there. I can't believe it! Last year the pair did return and cleaned out the remaining fecal sacs, but they never re-nested. Is she planning to start a third brood? By afternoon, when I peer into the nest there is a single blue-green egg; this time I look more closely and see that it is speckled with tiny brown spots.

Oh no! Here we go again—six more weeks of skulking among the rosebushes!

Wheet WHEET!

Curve-billed thrasher roots around the patio,
flings bark from garden to sidewalk,
smack-talking juvenile delinquent
        strews trash and
             tags the neighborhood,
his shrieks like rusty hinges on our backyard gate.
He rockets around the corner of the house
        pursuing his crony,
             barely misses my left ear.

If he discovers a western screech-owl
        sunning in its nest box doorway,
or spies a greater roadrunner attacking
        his hatchling offspring,
he does not back down.
With his screams, churrs, and feathery ruckus,
        owl drops back into the box,
        roadrunner scuttles,
             head hunched between shoulders.
With fluffed plumage, his triumphant look says,
If I could lift this middle feather on my wing. . . !

Thrasher flies to the cypress crown
        for a session of *wheet-WHEET*-ing,
elicits call-and-response from neighbors
        up the arroyo and down the street.

Then it is back to scrabbling
        among the bark bits,
            swinging his scythe-like beak,
        a grim reaper
seeking more grubby souls to harvest.

Creator of chaos, trasher of sidewalks,
        he drives my husband to frenzies
            of porch-sweeping.
Brash owner of sandy soil,
        bright, desiccated air,
            thorny chollas on which
        the unwary are crucified,
he probes with saber beak,
        glares with baleful yellow eyes.
Then, at dawn, he whispers
        an indescribably sweet and complex croon,
            like a saxophonist
                improvising,

as if he knows that this gritty scrap
        of New Mexico desert,
            this dawn of opal sky
        set in gold with fading diamonds,
is to be the stage upon which
        a singular blazing event is enacted—

resurrection of the sun.

Summer Sonnet

Midday saunter in summer is never
cool, sun blasts heavy from pale blistered sky.
I feel something like a sweaty fever,
mourning doves hunker down, too hot to fly.
Tomato and squash, though watered early,
wilt, under tuneless cicada screeching,
their leaves like limp rags, or crisp and curly.
But cottonwoods, downward toe tips reaching,
draw up water, offer cool dappled shade
in acequia dust my feet have stirred.
And ants, their tunneled formic cities laid
'neath hot sand, march in legions undeterred.
Animal and vegetable pray for rain,
peer hopefully at clouds but wait in vain.

What Does a Hummingbird Do When It Rains?

I had always imagined
a hummingbird huddled
    beneath a broad leaf
        or a stout branch
cringing from soaking rain drops
    until today

during a calm steady
    Navajo "female rain"
rufous hummingbird perches
ocotillo stalk tip
    bursts with tiny brilliant green leaves
    celebrating monsoon

he fans his tail
    blurs his wings but stays perched
dips his bill
    preens breast feathers
helicopters vertically
    a foot above the branch
returns
    repeats the exercise
raindrops glitter on fiery plumage

hummingbird takes a shower
that's what he does

Raven Heart

The raven perches, tilts his head,
ponders with corvid brain
the puzzles of existence,
or at least the test before him—
a piece of meat
dangling from a string.
Reaching down, he grasps
the knotted rope of mystery,
pulls it up,
clasps it beneath his feet,
reaches again, grasps and pulls,
until he attains the prize.
Watching him, I wonder
if only. . .

. . . if only I could fly with the raven,
I would raise my hands,
watch glistening midnight feathers
spring from my arms. I would
leap from this terrestrial life,
fling myself into the wind.

My companion,
a gleam in his bright eye,
croaks and folds his wings,
leads me in a barrel roll.
We double-twist,

plummet toward earth only to
flare our wings and
slingshot
back into the heavens.
We are of the sky,
of feathers and fire.
We love our lives,
know our enemies—
great horned owl, red-tailed hawk.
We plunge raucous,
mock their power.

Worries diminish
like my human life below.
Sun blazes on my ebony back,
wind rustles my feathers,
lifts my wings.
I open my mouth to
laugh but a joyous jumble of
gargles and knocks tumbles
from the black hatchet of my beak.

The knotted rope is unraveled.
Now I know how to live with
my human hands
and my raven heart.

CANTICLE TO CHANGE

Cottonwood leaves
flame out their final days
as glowing golden embers,
remnants of a burgeoning season.
Desiccated leaves cling,
rattle like bamboo wind-chimes

against pewter clouds,
until the day pitiless winds
tear them from their branches
to winter
under the feet of questing quail.

A sudden blur of wings
arrives at the last hummingbird feeder—
        hanging full,
            awaiting the late traveler.
Weary form perches,
        drinks deeply,

a bare patch of neck skin
testifies to near disaster—
            predator left with a clutch of feathers.
Black-chinned hummingbird has escaped,
only to face stress, lost energy, delays
in a season requiring
strength and endurance.
Is sugar water enough?

Life changes,
bones ache, joints grind,
muscles protest. Restless nights toss,
waves of heat flicker where there are no flames.
I confront the approach of
        winter.

Yet seasons
hold both departures—
        and arrivals.
As cottonwood leaves
spiral to the ground and hummingbirds
launch their improbable journeys,
transition
announces itself

with a sharp, emphatic
PINK!
and a querulous frosty whistle.
White-crowned sparrow
from mountainous northern realms
transforms these endings
into a lesson in beginnings.
Do not wait silently for winter to come,
prepare for a new season—
        a time of change,
        that warrants song.

SMALL THINGS

A black and purple bruise,
        night falls.
A young girl threads her way gingerly
across an ocean of grass
        dripping with dew,
air pungent with lilac,
beneath her feet the rasp
        of fresh-mown blades.
Cupped hands shelter a quiver
of feathers—the sparrow found stunned
        in a splash of window light.

Angry voices
slam into the screen door.
        The child flinches, melts among shadows.
Fear's acrid aroma rises
as she places the bird softly
        in a secret place
                beneath the lilacs.

From the attic of the world,
the goddess of small things watches,
        weeps star fire.
With a kiss from her cool silver lips
both girl and sparrow become

                invisible.

What I Know

I.
An insect-like rattle,
a ticking, hissing whisper in the grass,
a covert warble.
Tiny cryptic-feathered banjo player
picks scales with a bit of improvisation,
a recital for panther-spotted grasshoppers,
black-tailed jackrabbits, javelina, pronghorn,
secretive mate, and me.

He sings from feathery flag of cane bluestem
that nods above last year's grass clump,
leaves cured gold with cinnamon stripes by the sun,
a crackling quiver armed with new green arrows
fletched in the first July monsoon downpour.
He repeats his song,
listens to nearby call-and-response,
crouches forward,
flicks a single wing,
a kind of fluttering challenge.

I know this grasshopper sparrow—"D32"—
hot pink and black plastic bands on right leg
light blue and silver on left.
His nest beneath a tangled, grassy dome
        of sideoats grama cradles
        four brown-speckled eggs. One is pipping.

Territory encompasses
       mesquite upon whose spines loggerhead
         shrike has impaled a fence lizard
       cholla twisting beneath its crown of thorns
       a helix of rusty barbed wire.
A kingdom of grass.

II.
There are things recorded for science—
length of wing and beak, weight,
number of eggs and when they hatch.
But there are worlds to be known
that science cannot tell.

Science—
my career,
documentation of a sparrow's life,
real, true,
but only part of the truth.
Science is only the body
—skin and feathers, flesh and bones—
the rest is spirit and soul,
a mystery,
for which science has no words.

III.
Mysteries shimmer
beneath a blazing sun
       perhaps a mirage
       perhaps a dream.
How deciphered?
Where are the clues?

What would I ask of a grasshopper sparrow?

What are the words to your chittering song?
How did you clothe yourself
       in colors of sun-cured grass
             streaked with tanglehead's deep chestnut
       tobosa's silver gray, and sacaton's tawny tassels
             rabbitbrush's secret lemon yellow
     at corner of eye and bend of wing?
What shines behind your bright dark eye?
Do you share the cryptex code with your mate
       deep in the grass?
Does your heart break when the coachwhip
       flows away with the last of your nestlings?
Looking east as rose ribbons foretell
       the sun's resurrection,
west as monsoon clouds climb
       high above the Santa Ritas—

do you pray?

Corvid Cause

I.
the New Mexico winter sky is

raining
    crows

every October they arrive,
stream from across North America
for a black-feathered fiesta
in the sunny southwest,
frat brothers, sorority sisters who
did not make it to Florida or
Cabo San Lucas

II.
they wreak ebony mayhem
wherever they go—

        swagger in gangs across lawns,
        over McDonald's parking lots
        looking for French fries

        drip darkness from leaf-bare trees in
        broad daylight

execute trickster-dives on coyote,
who twists in jaw-snapping,
frenzied circles hoping to turn the tables,
snag one of his torturers

barrel-roll and rattle through the heavens,
harass red-tailed hawk, who drops
into cottonwoods, flails to maintain a perch
under cacophonous onslaught

midnight miasma of thousands
lifts from night roosts

black death on wings

III.
bright gaze of the joker
wild card
beyond roadkill-picking
raucous jabbering
crows flaunt piercing intelligence—

feathered seers revel in unmasking
disguised researchers who trap them,
remember, even when mask is worn by another

masterful impersonators, raucous mimes
imitate humans, machines,
mourning doves, sandhill cranes

native code-talkers
converse in crackling *caws*,
koaws, and *tocks*,
chortle rattling warnings

avian magician
performs stick tricks—
waves a small wand,
  reaches to the back of a box,
    pokes into a narrow tube,
  retrieves a chunk of meat—
a gold coin from his jet-black sleeve

Merlin, the wizard—
transmogrified by an obsidian cloak
sidles warily along a branch

black magic, the good kind

Ornithologist's Oracle

Atop my antique writing desk,
erected as a shrine before which
I read poems and write every morning,
a company of keepsakes,
rainbow-hued Butterfly Dancer kachina,
badger fetish looking out from carnelian eyes,
oval-framed picture of my grandmother,
> *Portrait of a Young Woman*
> with her Vermeer smile,
> hair tied back in a huge white bow,
vanilla candle in Turkish tea glass, and
a porcelain figurine.

> When I was very young,
> living in Amsterdam,
> photos in a now-dusty album capture
> > my mischievous eyes gleaming
> > from a tumble of dark ringlets.
> When we left for the States,
> a family friend presented me with
> a Hummel figurine.
> She has traveled with me, across years,
> nestled in a box, in closet depths.

I have experienced one by one,
loss of parents, other loved ones, mentors.
Perhaps I grasped—
before they could slip through my fingers—
mementos tied to mysteries.

Only now, after fifty years,
do I recognize figurine as oracle.
First glimpsed
by a curly-haired three-year-old,
a prophetic image glimmers—
     a young girl leans against a fence,
     a look of wonder on her face,
     her porcelain finger points
     to a small blue bird
     perched on a fence post.

THERE

Hope is the thing with feathers
That perches in the soul,
And sings the tune without the words,
And never stops at all, . . .

—Emily Dickinson

HERE AND THERE

today
I occupy
a creaking chair
on the patio, drink coffee,
surrounded by rapidly warming
New Mexico desert morning, a sparrow
whispers a monotonous chatter, immediately
drowned out by cicadas tuning up for an afternoon
chorus of screeching while cottonwoods swish their skirts

today I am here but dream of a steamy Madagascar morning,
world's largest island floats in the Indian Ocean, there
ground-rollers whoop, giant cockroaches hiss,
tenrecs snuffle their pointy noses among
leaves, and black and white sifakas
in fur coats dance through
feathery branches, sing
to me a Malagasy
serenade

both here
and there—I pay
attention

Archaeopteryx

We praise you, amazing *Archaeopteryx*,
for this wondrous radiation of birds,
multitudinous rays of soaring, flapping, wingèd light.

From between layers of limestone
your twisted fossilized form evolved
        prehistory,
transformed itself into feathered hordes,
speaks to us from rocky resting places.
From your extended wings, serpentine neck,
petrified tail, stony curved claws, and
saw-toothed smile have sprung myriads.

What drove you from the bonds of earth
into the heavens?
Did your sturdy cursorial legs and feet,
revolutionary broad, rounded wings propel you—
like roadrunners and secretarybirds—
        in pursuit of speedy insects, small lizards
        and scurrying mammals?
Or did you employ wing-claws to scramble skyward—
like hoatzins and young turacos—
        from branch to branch, to leap,
        then glide from above onto oblivious prey?
From transformative adaptations
in your crow-sized form,
no one could have imagined—

albatross soars aloft for months above the sea on
                twelve-foot glider spans,
        hummingbird hovers before a penstemon with
                tiny helicopter-rotors,
        and peregrine falcon stoops
                at 200 miles per hour on scimitar wings.
Who doesn't dream of flying?

What was your contribution to the cosmic symphony?
With serrated grin—did you sing?
        ethereal fluted harmony of solitaire?
        improvisational croon of thrasher?
        tympanic drumming of ruffed grouse?
        or perhaps, more likely, dissonant screech
        of parakeet or mocking clatter of crow?
With trouser-feathered legs—did you dance?
        Jacksonian moonwalk, finger-snapping
                wrists of manakin?
        elegant bowing, pirouetting ballet of crane?
        foot-stomping, burbling square-dance
                of prairie-chicken, or blue suede swagger and
        beak-pointing disco moves of booby?
Your musical score and choreography,
        your performance,
                in Jurassic jazz time signature.

What is your legacy?
conquest of the heavens,
throngs of descendants,
rainbow-colored plumes,
shapes beyond belief,

pierce universal darkness,
illuminate our imaginations.

We embrace
feathered icons of culture and spirituality
  raven—lifter of first human from a clam shell
  Horus—falcon-headed Egyptian god
    of sky and kingship
  Andean condor—messenger to Inca gods
  brolga—dancing embodiment of Australian
    aboriginal creativity
  red-crowned crane—Asian emblem
    of longevity and good luck
characters that make us laugh
  Heckle and Jeckle, Woody Woodpecker,
  Donald Duck, Tweety Bird, Road Runner,
  Woodstock, Blu and Jewel, Angry Birds
the spectacle of beauty and abundance
  red knot hordes feast on horseshoe crab eggs
    in Delaware Bay
  rivers of raptors flow over Veracruz
  legions of warblers pour
    from boreal forest nurseries
  hosts of sandhill cranes gargle and dance
    on the Platte River
and the comfort of backyard birds
  robins, cardinals, chickadees, jays, thrashers,
  finches, wrens, doves, swallows, flycatchers,
  warblers, blackbirds.

Oh, *Archaeopteryx*,
not a frozen, fossilized image
impressed into a sedimentary stronghold,
but the wonder of a living, evolving being that
seized the wind with feathered wings,
grasped the slippery prey of the past in toothy jaws,
and clawed its way through time and space—
beyond extinction.

FEATHER MITES II

manakin moonwalk
on back-stepping gold thighs
wing snap tips red cap

cisticola sings from sky halo
falls from heaven

long-tailed ground-roller
crest raised, tail cocked, blue-masked
Madagascar's
long-lost cousin
to my desert roadrunner

unseen piha
among rainforest leaves
only the scream

yesterday lyrebird imitated
kookaburra chatter
today chainsaw racket

infectious laughter
kookaburra cackles
at his own joke

protea flower
opens bowl of sweetness
sugarbird takes a sip

masked-weaver nest created
without opposable thumbs
round basket woven
with ribbons of grass
planet held by a thread

Sacred Rites

Sailboat anchor-chains and rigging clank,
creaking docks ride soft swells.
Across the inlet kingfisher perches
on driftwood, cackles
satisfaction at having
filched another fish from the lake.

Dawn air is cold and still,
mist settles over the water,
obscures spectral twins
anchored beneath every boat,
tree reflections along the shore.

A ghostly priestess glides in,
low over the lake.
She executes an ungainly landing,
combination of comedy and grace,
blue-gray robes settle about her shoulders,
a mantle of tranquility.

The feathered phantom watches from across the water.
Satisfied, she folds her neck,
                        stalks
lifts   each   leg
freezes   a moment
            unleashes
        the harpoon of her bill
among reeds and oily reflections.

Harpoon retrieved—empty—an unanswered prayer,
heron lifts from the water's edge with a croak,
ponderously at first,
drawing dangling legs and
priestly robes behind her.

A power boat roars.
Mirror images of the morning
disperse in a million glittering bits of wave.

Gyrfalcon

I still remember her
on the Great Plains of Colorado
far from her Arctic home
pale-feathered pilgrim
from land of ice and snow
        perched on a telephone pole—

I knew what she was.

When she mounted the sky
she left us with a falcon-shaped emptiness.
It was not enough
—we wanted more.
We clambered back into the car
raced north, then west, madly
searching, stopped
scanned the horizon

leaden sky, full of wind
only a few Canada geese winging their way
south from the reservoir.
Then they broke formation
with wild evasive maneuvers
dove and twisted—

I knew she was there.

She came in silent
a feathered missile
high, from behind and above
she struck
talons like a pair of brass knuckles.
Twice her weight, the goose crumpled,
     limp,
             plummeted to earth—

I knew her power.

Gyrfalcon descended to earth
stood upon
what had been a goose.
She plucked feathers and down
tore flesh and ate
     in the stubble of an empty cornfield,
with blood on her beak.
Beneath her fierce gaze—

I knew her.

The Plunge

Small black-and-white-checkered ship,
the loon sails Muscongus Sound,
     through smooth pewter water
        laced with ribbons of aquamarine and gold.
His snowy prow
    slices the bay,
       trailing multi-colored shards
    in a V-shaped wake
that washes pebbles
on some distant shore.

From coal-black visage
     rubies glow, squeezed from silver alewives'
       slender throats. Fresh from a dive to
    the icy deep, his wild ululation
rends my garments, drags my soul from
     wherever it was sleeping. With upward thrust
      below my tenth rib, iron dagger
    bill pierces my heart,
plunges with me
to the depths.

Living with Otus

Nothing on my "to do" list was as important as spending a few hours alone, enjoying the back patio on a warm, mid-October afternoon. With a cushion, iced tea, and a book, I settled in the shade below the *latillas*. After fifteen minutes, I stopped reading, and looked up into the eyes of a western screech-owl.

Perched less than five yards away on a wisteria branch among bright green leaves and dappled sunlight, it was the first western screech-owl I had seen on our property. Torn between documenting the event and enjoying the gift of the owl's presence, I snuck inside long enough to grab my camera. Not satisfied with my first pictures, I crept closer—the owl seemed unfazed, even when I crouched on top of the patio table! I stayed on the patio for a couple hours, reading (not much), and watching the owl; sometimes it watched me and sometimes its eyes drifted into slits. At dusk, facing out toward the back yard, it watched whatever it is that owls watch, and eventually launched silently into the growing darkness.

That might have been the end of the story, but I was intrigued! Where had the screech-owl come from? Was it male or female? The sexes are not distinguishable by plumage. When I broached the subject of putting up a nest box, my husband Dave pointed out that the owl would likely never return. However, he eventually succumbed to my "if we build it they will come" argument. In late October I propped a ladder against our cottonwood, found the perfect spot facing southeast (and visible from our dining room window), and mounted a screech-owl nest box against the trunk.

I climbed down, and we waited. Eventually, resigned to failure, I clung to my habit of checking the box, looking for something other than an empty hole.

December 26 was a bright, frigid day. Sticking my head out the back door to see how cold it was, I unconsciously glanced at the nest box. I almost tripped over the door jamb—there was a screech-owl sticking its head out of the hole! Belated Merry Christmas! As I had hoped, by orienting the nest box so the opening faced southeast, a screech-owl was encouraged to select it for a winter roost. They perch in cavity openings on cold days to soak up the warmth of the sun.

And so, it began. The story unfolded over the next several years. Western screech-owls are residents and often return to reuse the same nest cavity or nest box. In subsequent years a screech-owl would appear sometime in November or December to roost in the box for the winter. We started calling the owl "Otus," which is the former screech-owl genus and lends itself more easily to nicknames than does the current *Megascops*. As an ornithologist, and in the hope that there would be an interesting story to tell, I began keeping an informal "owl journal"—dates and observations—and placed the *Birds of North America* western screech-owl species account near the back door to look up the things I didn't know. For the rest of the winter we watched "him." He sat in the entrance to the box ignoring us, even when greeted cheerfully with, "Hi Otus!" Sometimes Otus would be visible in the nest box opening all day; other times we'd only see him for a few minutes at dusk. As the days lengthened, Otus left the box later in the evening to forage. Soon, neighbor birds discovered the owl. The greater roadrunner perched on the patio wall, bill-rattling—Otus dropped to the bottom of the box. Other birds—bushtits, dark-eyed juncos, lesser goldfinches, house finches—regularly scolded and mobbed the owl. As winter brightened toward spring and showed no sign of a second screech-owl, we began to wonder whether Otus would find a mate. Our sand sage habitat some distance from the Río Grande, with only one large tree, was not exactly prime habitat.

5 February: screech-owl observed calling from the nest box and nearby perches

In early March, I noticed that when I passed near the nest box, Otus would get all "squinchy"—my term for alarmed screech-owl behavior—transforming himself from a fluffy ball with golden globes for eyes into a skinny streak of feathers with eyes squeezed shut in order to look like a stick. I was surprised, because Otus had seemed accustomed to us. Later in the month, working in the front yard, I had an unexplained urge to peer among the prickly branches of a scraggly Arizona cypress. Face-to-face with a screech-owl, it took me five seconds to remember that I had just seen an owl in the box. The mystery of "squinchy Otus" was solved—it was a female, who was not yet accustomed to her un-feathered neighbors! We called her "Ophelia."

Otus and Ophelia started their family. One evening in late March I watched Ophelia fly from the nest box to one of her favorite perches on top of the flycatcher nest box in the back yard. She sat quietly until Otus joined her. They nibbled each other's bills. Otus called with soft rapid, multiple toots and Ophelia responded with higher-pitched toots. Then Otus fluttered up onto Ophelia's back and they copulated. It would be too much to call it ecstasy, but it was more than momentary. Otus perched on her back for perhaps 10 seconds, then flew to a nearby tree. Ophelia remained for a minute or so, then took off into the dusk.

Screech-owls will call regularly at night in late winter, but Otus and Ophelia were practically silent. We rarely saw both of them at the same time. Most likely their silence acknowledged the presence of the larger predatory great horned owls that we occasionally observed. Unlike the great horned owls, Cooper's hawks are diurnal hunters, but also consider small owls a nice meal. One day a large Cooper's hawk crouched beneath the bird feeder devouring a mourning dove that she had snatched. When I looked up into the wisteria, Otus was cowering high in the vegetation with his face turned into the corner, hiding the part of him that might not blend into the shadows— his eyes. The real danger was demonstrated six years later when one of the naive young owls of that year was killed by a Cooper's hawk. In contrast to the hawk, Otus was a "sit and wait" predator, watching motionless from favorite perches, especially the wisteria vine where I had seen him that first afternoon or the top of the flycatcher nest box. When he saw something interesting, he stood on tiptoe and swiveled his head in a kind of clockwise circle to triangulate on the target. Then he would drop down on the beetle or mouse from above.

One day Ophelia, perched in the nest box opening, repeatedly stretched her neck, opened her beak wide, and closed it. I was mystified, until something appeared in her mouth, she leaned out of the box, and a pellet dropped to the ground! Dried up, regurgitated pellets containing all the undigestible bits of a meal had appeared on the patio before, but I had never seen one produced. I scurried out to retrieve the pellet. Dave noted that only a biologist would dream of such behavior! Anyway, it was still warm, a bit sticky, and had a sort of pungent-but-not-offensive smell. Thus began my owl-pellet-collection-project. In winter, pellets contained tiny pieces of mouse bones; in summer, they were dry and crumbly, composed primarily of beetle parts. Someday those zip-lock baggies of pellets will be useful in writing a paper about the western screech-owl's diet.

I was never able to confirm egg laying or incubation initiation dates—screech-owl secrets hidden away inside the nest box. There was no owl at the nest box entrance for a while and I wondered if Ophelia was sitting on eggs. A female screech-owl usually lays three to five eggs and does all the incubation; she leaves the nest to defecate, cough up a pellet, or hunt for a short period. While Ophelia incubated, Otus roosted nearby.

By May hatching seemed likely. Ophelia hung so far out of the nest box opening that I feared she'd fall out—perhaps the box was full of hatchlings? Then one May morning, I shivered in the chilly dawn darkness, watching, waiting, and listening. I heard the single soft toot of a nearby screech-owl. Suddenly Otus flew directly into the nest box, eliciting high-pitched twittering.

23 May: at least one screech-owl egg has hatched

27 May: owlet stuck his head out of nest box this morning

As Ophelia continued to tend the nestlings, Otus roosted gradually closer and closer to the nest box as fledging time approached. By the first of June, the gray, fuzzy face of an owlet frequently peered out of the nest box opening, looking surprised. Scrabbling sounds came from the box, suggesting there was more than one hatchling. Otus was harassed mercilessly by thrashers. At feeding time, a nestling would hang out of the hole, bobbing up and down until Otus or Ophelia fluttered in front to transfer some tidbit of food.

5 June: fledging occurred last night; one owlet perched
tightly against trunk of cottonwood near nest box in the a.m.

The owlet(s) fledged at approximately the same time
both years. I looked up how long egg incubation and
hatching-to-fledging takes in screech-owls. Ophelia
probably laid eggs the first week of April and hatching
likely occurred in the first week of May.

In the first year, we saw a single fledgling occasionally
during the first week. Then it was gone (or unseen) all
summer; we suspected that it had not survived. However,
one morning in late August a young owl sat on the rim of
the bird bath bill-snapping at me.

The second year was a different story. On a windy June
morning, I saw a fledged owlet clinging to a cottonwood
branch, in danger of being tossed from its safe harbor.
In the afternoon a white-tailed antelope squirrel trilled
loudly from the patio. First glance revealed an adult
screech-owl perched on the light fixture, while the
squirrel crouched below trilling, its tail quivering with
indignation. Then I saw the real cause of the ruckus—
the owl fledgling was on the ground. It had been blown
down (fortunately inside the patio walls). The owlet
toddled on surprisingly long legs over to the base of the
wisteria and crammed itself among the roots. We were
pleased with another successful owl nesting effort.

10 June: TWO owl fledglings on the porch!

13 June: OMG, THREE owlets on the porch with Otus and Ophelia!

And so, on the eighth day—miracle of miracles—the complete fledged family was revealed! Because screech-owls do not hatch on the same day, "our" owlets were significantly different sizes. One fledgling was really large—likely a female (usually larger). Another appeared to be "the runt," probably the last to hatch and a smaller male.

Otus and Ophelia were attentive parents; one of them was always present with the owlets in their patio playpen. The curve-billed thrashers kept close tabs on the screech-owls' whereabouts. They seemed to take the owls' presence as a personal affront; their angry *churr*s and *wheet WHEET*s resounded regularly. Occasionally there were pitched battles. A skirmish in the wisteria resulted in a thrasher crashing out of the tangle looking very disheveled (but alive) and Otus dropping down to perch on a patio chair. One night as it got almost too dark to see, a fledgling curve-billed thrasher innocently pecked about below the peanut feeder. I barely had time to murmur, "Oh, baby, you better find a safe roost for the night!" when Ophelia took a pass at it. It was a miss, but there was a whole lot of *wheet WHEET*-ing from thrasher parents and more unsuccessful passes by Ophelia.

Throughout the summer we were entertained by the goofy appearance and antics of the "three stooges." The fledglings' juvenal plumage was fluffy and loose. Their most obvious difference from Otus and Ophelia was the horizontal whitish-gray and black barring on their breasts and heads, instead of the adult vertical streaking. The youngsters had little in the way of feathered "horns," although as they got older the fuzz stuck up a bit like ears.

They communicated in soft squeaking, twittery voices and they were very curious. In childish imitation of an adult owl's triangulation behavior, I watched the kids bobbin' and weavin' in the most ridiculous manner. Owlets perched on any vaguely horizontal surface, often  fluttering and teetering precariously. When flying they appeared light on the wing, but the conclusion of these flights was often less than graceful. One landed with a crash in the middle of a large potted plant and clambered out with wings akimbo and feathers awry!

The owlets loved the birdbath; fluttering puffballs perched on the rim and took turns walking around in the water. Occasionally one used the birdbath for its intended purpose, ruffling its feathers and thrashing about. They practiced "hunting," repeatedly attacking large pieces of unsuspecting bark mulch, which they carried about, and then attempted to dismember. Often these "victims" were found floating in the birdbath in the morning, apparently found wanting in the taste, digestibility, or nutrition department.

I watched one youngster fly up to the clothesline and wobble there, inspecting the row of washed plastic bags clipped there to dry. On another occasion an owlet flew to the clothesline where it nibbled at the clothespins, yanked at the waistband of my shorts, and pooped on my jeans!

> 20 July: whole family roosts regularly on back porch;
> owlets perch on patio chairs, flower pots, barbecue grill,
> blue boot brush, porch light

Indeed, we discovered that hosting an owl family is not for "neat-niks." Between the poop coming out of one end and the pellets out of the other, they are messy. It was easy to identify their favorite roost sites. We eventually gave up on keeping the porch floor and the grill cover clean. The potted fig seedling looked a bit burned from the extra fertilizer.

As August got hotter, the family regularly roosted during the day on various empty pots stacked on an old baker's rack on the patio. They panted and exhibited a behavior known as "gular flutter," in which they flutter the skin in their throats as an additional way to cool off through evaporation. It was too hot up in the wisteria with the sun baking down from above. The shade beneath the *latillas* offered respite from 90- to 100-degree F temperatures.

25 August: owlets beginning to molt out of juvenal plumage—bars on breast changing to vertical streaks

I like to think that the parents had decided we were basically harmless. When the family was perched on the back porch, we could not always avoid going out into the patio. There were, after all, plants to water and brats to barbecue. Quietly opening the back door, we walked softly, kept our eyes cast down, and crept around the bushes to avoid threatening the owlets perched on the flower pots. Occasionally they "went squinchy," or puffed up their feathers and snapped their bills. Mostly they just watched.

15 September: adults perched in wisteria over back porch; no sign of owlets for some time

The young screech-owls had dispersed to find territories and homes of their own. I told our neighbors that this would be a good time to mount a screech-owl nest box if they were ready for some slightly messy owlish entertainment.

In the meantime, it was autumn, and it was time to put down my book and iced tea again, this time for a "to do" list that included: hose down the porch, prop the ladder against the cottonwood, lift the trapdoor on the side of the nest box, scoop out the remains of haphazard owl housekeeping, and toss a handful of fresh wood shavings into the box in preparation for the coming winter.

Owl Dreams

In the predawn glimmer
the screech-owl perches on her post,
old woman in a moth-eaten overcoat.
Soft bouncing hoots ruffle the feathers at her throat.

I slip into violet shadows,
        a breeze lifts the hair from my forehead.
Spicy scent of wet sand sage
        tiptoes softly across the back of my tongue—
        morning-after-rain smells like chai tea tastes.
A thrasher croons from the rooftop—
        Billie Holiday husking the blues
                from the dark smoky depths of a club
                        somewhere in Harlem.

Early morning chill
        traces cold steel down my spine, drags me back
to the owl's wild gaze.
The diminutive huntress reaches for me,
        beak stained with mouse blood
rips into my soul—
        owl and human exchange skins.

        I fly by instinct at midnight with terrible gaze,
        seeking warm-blooded prey—
        the plunge, the shriek, the crunch of tiny bones,
        the sweet horror of my fierceness,
        the not-so-gentle justice of clenched talons
        soaked with blood.

I plummet back into my body,
my human heart pounds.
As the sun stirs, throws off the blanket of night,
the owl's twin golden orbs flame for an instant,
     an owlish cry claws at my throat,
          as she unfurls the cloak of her wings and
              disappears into my dreams.

In daylight and darkness—
I will remember her.
     An iron taste rasps my tongue.

BLACK SWIFTS

Slicing their way
   across the sky,
      ebony scythes reap
         the wind, pierce the veil
      of Jemez Falls, reach
   their nests plastered
on dripping stone walls;
   black swifts come
      and go all summer,
         beaks full of insects
      for chicks in the mist.
   Autumn arrives—
they are gone.

Now we know,
   the horned moon leads them;
      black-feathered boomerangs,
         carve air across 7000 kilometers,
      harvest clouds of insects
   in the deepest Amazon.
In spring—they return to the
   same waterfall that flung them
      south eight months ago—earth,
         feathers, water, wind, insects
      and tiny beating hearts
   of swift flyers the
color of midnight.

From the Ashes

Beneath dripping rainforest canopy,
resplendent quetzal
lives a tropical mystery—
    forages among fruit-laden foliage,
    flies from branch to branch beneath tree tops,
    folds himself into a nest cavity—
crowned in feathered coronet,
    arrayed in fantastic emerald train,
        ruby vestments.
Phoenix of the tropics—
    not consumed on the funeral pyre
        of reincarnation but transformed
    in the maelstrom, reborn on the wheel of life—
blood and phosphorescent fire.

In dawn mist,
before the sun opens its eye
above Sierra Madre de Chiapas,
from a dense dark cauldron of
    vines, blue morphos,
        jaguars and fer de lances,
the quetzal erupts into smoky air
    trailing ribbons of emerald flame,
wild cries carry him across the sky,
back into a teeming
primordial dream.

What I was—falls away—
not as ashes carried into the sun,
        but embers of my former self
                borne into steamy jungle.

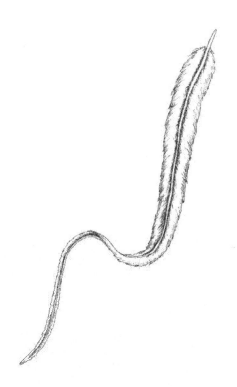

As If They Were Not There

We fly, easily, south across political borders to Veracruz and Oaxaca, Mexico, to partake of a visual and auditory feast, an ornithological orgy of feathered messengers who defy boundaries, both physical and political. We marvel at the beauty and diversity of birds—large and small, resplendently plumaged and subtly brown, familiar and strange. Some live their entire lives south of "our" borders—great curassow, bare-throated tiger-heron, azure-crowned hummingbird, scarlet macaw, green shrike-vireo, crimson-collared tanager. For two-thirds of the year they live side-by-side with migratory birds. Both consume food from the same neotropical menu— nectar, insects fleeing ant swarms, exotic fruits, fish, and seeds; they share habitats that produce these bountiful banquets—from sere tropical deciduous forest to dripping rainforest and mangrove swamp, grassland to montane coniferous forest. Then, leaving wintering grounds, swallow-tailed kite, ruby-throated hummingbird, barn swallow, hermit thrush, orange-crowned warbler, and summer tanager wing across mountains, plains, seas, and walls, biannual immigrants, to gorge on summer plenty and breed in the U.S. and Canada—these birds we call "ours" for one-third of the year. On the wheel of life, in the circle of seasons, walls are meaningless. Ancient biological demands of avian migration roll over physical obstacles as if they were not there.

We live in a country comprised of people from many places and cultures—some have been here since before written history, some migrated here with dreams, others dragged here in nightmares. All faced cultural, physical, and political obstacles. Where we succeed in welcoming, sharing, and understanding our differences—taste of kimchi and curry, music of oud and kalimba, spectacle of corn dance and Japanese Noh, love of whatever god we worship—diversity tantalizes our senses, arouses imagination, and ravishes our hearts.

Walls of steaming rice divide
the platter, separate three thick pools,
chunks of chicken swim in Oaxacan *mole*, a spread
for the senses,
a feast reminiscent of feathery hues—
    almendrado, creamy blonde head
        of chestnut-colored woodpecker,
    coloradito, rich red deeper
        than hepatic tanager wings,
    negro, the bittersweet chocolate-brown of
        Sumichrast's wren.

Rice walls stand, built kernel by kernel
in a kitchen roiling with spicy aromas
and savory broths—
        to make a visual impression,
        separate color and flavor,
        facilitate taste comparison.

But barricades must fall.
Tearing down, consuming walls
saturated in almonds, chiles, or chocolate
is part of the gustatory experience.
Unavoidable mélange
  sweet and sharp, dark and bright,
    dips and flutters in my nose like swallows,
yellow with red, and red with black
  swirl and marble, eddy and merge
    in rivulets on my tongue,
  like rivers of migrating raptors above
the Isthmus of Tehuantepec—

  a miracle.

CISTICOLIDAE (FAMILY)

Genus: Cisticola
—*after Sylvia Legris' poem "Papulæ (Order I.)"*

on a scale from Tiny to Stout,
Foxy to Pale-crowned, Rock-loving to Cloud,
african ecological equivalent of
Passerellidae (sparrows in a new world),
cryptic little brown bits,
neither resplendent nor Boran,
but Neddicky, Madagascan, Levaillant's.

o, the diverse, distinctive Trilling variations
on a theme of cisticola!

consider the Zitting, the Wailing,
spokes of the sylvioid radiation of oscines,
the Singing repeats among the Hunter's,
the Croaking, the Wing-snapping,
the Bubbling.

neither *haesitatus* nor *troglodytes*,
like an orchestra of musicians
in the grass, scratching and Whistling
a covert overture,
the *anonymus, aberrans, galactotes*,
all the instruments of the percussion section
—Winding, Rattling, Tinkling, even Chattering—

dressed in Long-tailed coats,
dueting like dueling ngonis
Ashy in the Desert,
Golden-headed angels
of *aridulus* savanna grasslands.

—this poem plays with the common names
(capitalized), and scientific species names (italicized)
of cisticola species.

CASSOWARY

From dark, leafy undergrowth
like a fantastic rainforest dream
he pushes aside foliage
emerges on burly legs
strides on feet with dagger claws that can
eviscerate a man

> *or a woman, presumably.*
> *The sight of his primeval form*
> *evacuates my lungs.*

As tall as my shoulder,
he is robed in wiry plumage
that flows like long, coarse horsehair.
His head, crowned with a bony casque
twisted to one side, bears scars from
muscling through thickets,
> battling other cassowaries.

> *My breathless mind scrabbles*
> *with trembling fingers for images*
> *to fix in memory*
> *for my lifetime, the future—*
> *of which the cassowary may not be a part.*

Nature's "paint-by-number" brushwork—
his head and brawny neck, cerulean and aquamarine

born of island sky and ocean,
folded scarlet flesh rolls down his nape,
crimson drips from his wattle,
reflects watermelon flesh
that lured him from the rainforest,

blood pounding through my arteries.

Masterpiece of the late Cretaceous,
threatened by the Anthropocene.

Accustomed to humans,
he brushes past me, feathers whispering.

I could—
touch him.
I don't.
I stand,
a statue of myself.

He preens,
casque scrapes sandpapery through feathers.
He turns.
For a moment,
his great red-brown eyes scrutinize—
alien awareness
an electric shock!
Then he walks away.

For years into the future,
I gaze into my sand sage desert,
      burn with his fierce and ancient
           knowing.

EVERYWHERE

Imagine the marsh wren making himself
inside his own dream. Imagine the wren,
created by the marsh, inside the marsh
of his own creation, unaware of his being
inside this dream of mine where I imagine
he dreams within the boundaries of his own
fixed black eye around which this particular
network of glistening weeds and knotted
grasses and slow-dripping gold mist
and seeded winds shifting in waves of sun
turns and tangles and turns itself completely
inside out again here composing me
in the stationary silence of its only existence.

—Pattiann Rogers, "The Dream of the Marsh
Wren: Reciprocal Creation"

CACOPHONOUS LOVE SONG

Robins, goldfinches, downy woodpeckers—
I was satisfied with domestic, maple-shaded lawns
and backyard birds until Panama.

Now I want new, exotic birds,
wild unfamiliar landscapes—multiple worlds
from which to choose. Steamy neotropics,
towering trees puncture rainforest canopies,
grasp thin soil with their toes, drip moisture,
damp arms draped in vines and orchids reach
for blare of equatorial sun, offer a universe
to emerald tree boas, poison dart frogs,
yellow-throated euphonias, and band-backed wrens.
Misty shadows camouflage furtive felines,
felt, but never seen.

At dawn, beneath steady drips from yesterday's
drenching afternoon thunderstorm,
amidst constant whine of unrepelled mosquitos,
howler monkeys growl, great curassows boom,
chachalacas screech in harmony, and army ants
swarm the forest floor, flush insects
to be snapped up by a skittering, flittering
mixed flock of birds that scribbles
scratchy love letters to ornithologists
among ceiba trees and lianas,
assassin bugs and epiphytes—

white-plumed antbirds, black-spotted bare-eyes,
red-throated ant-tanagers, ruddy woodcreepers.

Coming, going, always seeking,
I save sultry valentines,
pack and unpack.
Each time a piece of me
does not come back.

When I Stop Counting

As a research ornithologist and backyard birder in North America (here) and an international birder around the globe (there), I frequently count birds, record notes on field sheets, and create rather dry lists. But when I stop counting for a moment and pay attention, I have witnessed avian wonders, comedies, and riddles everywhere.

1

The female roadrunner skulked past; a pursuing male stopped, glared, and raised his crest and tail simultaneously in cartoonish manner. I pointed, "She went that way." As he disappeared, nearby movement caught my eye. The female roadrunner played a slow game of "ring-around-the-red yucca" with a cottontail. When the bird stopped, the rabbit reinitiated a hopping orbital pursuit! They circled the yucca at least ten times. Finally, bird got bored (or dizzy) and slunk off with her head hunched between shoulders. . . .

2

Motoring across icy water in a Boston Whaler, we surveyed winter birds by boat on Gunston Cove off the Potomac River. We paused to count a crowd of loafing gulls on a sandbar. Panning my binoculars slowly through the birds, 20 . . . 30 . . . 35 ring-billed gulls, 10

. . . 15 . . . 17 herring gulls. . . I stopped abruptly and panned back. A renegade herring gull sauntered among his cronies hefting a bright yellow tennis ball in his beak!

3

A sparrow flushed from beneath our feet in Arizona's desert grasslands. It fluttered toward the safety of a swale, but a sharp-shinned hawk plunged out of nowhere, snagged the sparrow on the wing. Before the small accipiter could savor the tasty bite, a larger northern harrier stooped on the "sharpie" who dropped the victim! Neither recovered the lucky sparrow.

4

After a cool morning in the field chasing sparrows, I spent a sweaty afternoon in front of a laptop entering field data. There was no AC in the casita, just a box fan to redistribute hot air and curtains over the door to block late afternoon sunlight. Fluttering shadows danced across the curtains. Curve-billed thrashers nested in a nearby cholla; I wondered why they were flitting and *churr*-ing when everyone else was resting in the shade. Not really thinking, I pushed the door open. A 3-foot western diamondback flowed slowly across the porch, also looking for shade!

5

Roadrunners are innovative hunters. These predators will consume anything they can get their beaks on—stunned goldfinch below a window, squawking thrasher baby scared out of its nest, or hapless young quail that zigged when it should have zagged. On this morning, a sharp clattering alerted me to a roadrunner whacking a mousetrap back and forth against the ground, attempting to extricate a dead mouse!

6

While preparing a fancy backpackers' breakfast in Rocky Mountain National Park, we realized neither of us had packed oil for the frying pan. The just-add-water pancakes were more than a bit on the dry, crusty side, providing our minimum daily requirement of carbon! When a gray jay sailed silently out of the trees and made off with the crumbly black half of one field kitchen experiment, we were surprised, but not too upset. Now I know why gray jays are called "camp robbers."

7

Smaller than some hummingbirds and the weight of four paperclips, bushtits are the tiniest birds in these desert shrublands. Their nests, lacy socks hung from tree branches, are crocheted of spider webs and plant materials. This season "our" pair settled for a substitute—the frayed ends of a nylon rope binding wisteria to porch post, its snow-white fibers sticking out like Einstein's hair. The bushtits employed a novel strategy: grasp a nylon strand and fly. Because the fiber was still attached, each bird quickly "reached the end of its rope" and swung down like a tiny feathered pendulum, using its weight to break the thread. The plan worked one time out of ten and she (or he) flew away with the loot. The other nine times, bushtit dropped stubborn strand, picked another, and tried again.

8

Male satin bowerbirds are meticulous Australian architects and interior designers. Near our campsite, a male finalized construction details in hope of impressing a prospective mate. His bower was an arched walkway of twigs. Surrounding landscape was decorated with objects that caught his beady dark blue eye—blue plastic straws, blue bits of potato chip bags, blue pen and bottle caps. The bowerbird conducted a detailed inspection, perhaps comparing it to the blueprint in his head. Dissatisfied with the placement of one stick, he pulled it out, walked the circumference, stabbed it in at a new location, shook his head, pulled it, carried it through the bower and poked it elsewhere, stepped back and cocked his head. Apparently satisfied with the renovation, he flew off in search of yet another perfect blue lawn ornament.

9

I was tired of rain, mosquitos, and being nice to the rest of our birding group. Grumpy and damp, I began walking on gridded trails back to camp in Peru's Amazon rainforest. Around a corner, everything changed. Twenty-five meters ahead, a flock of 12 pale-winged trumpeters trotted along like large black chickens sporting white rumps. Sun had broken through soggy skies. The trumpeters, using the path as a jungle highway, stopped in a single patch of sunlight, crouched, spread their wings to dry, and then ambled on. After ten minutes, they slipped off the trail into thick undergrowth.

10

In Brazil's wondrous Atlantic rainforest some mysteries are better than others. Below the research station, a black-and-white hawk-eagle soared across the slope. It landed in a treetop along a ridgeline. It flapped wings, spread tail, and tumbled forward on the branch while holding on with its talons. Hanging upside-down, it fluttered and fanned its tail for a couple seconds, then let go, dropped into flight, and was gone over the ridge! Only sometimes do I understand what I see.

Feather Mites III

petals fly
canaries mine gold
in garden daisies

crow can't get no satisfaction
coal-black thoughts

clouds to wind
swallow stitching
quilt full of feathers

beneath tree steeple
vault of leaves
dove on branch
folds her wings
amen

                    commas
                    released from my poems
                    sparrows on barbed wire

CATALOG OF AVIAN AMAZEMENT

I have a feathered dream
that you will share with me, perhaps,
this wingèd paean of gratitude
for the wonders,
the messengers that are birds.

Beaks of birds in every shape, evolved to
capture prey of all shapes and sizes, but also
to feed chicks, preen feathers, and bill mates.
Oh, praise hammering wedge of woodcreeper,
probing rapier of crane, crook'd, upside-down
sieve of flamingo, insect-picking tweezers of
warbler, flesh-tearing hook of falcon, scimitar
curve of curlew, expandable fish-purse
of pelican, nectar-sipping straw of hummingbird,
seed-crushing vice of finch, salt-spraying
tubenose of storm-petrel, cone-prying adaptation
of crossbill, while merganser and penguin
retain the serrated grin of dinosaur ancestors
for grasping slippery fishy prey.

Broad wings and splayed primary tips of condor
bear us above the squalid smallness of earth,
only to plunge us back into the fray—
all of us tied to this earth for good and evil,
life and death. Hearts rejoice in stubby flippers
of puffin flying beneath the sea, tympani-
drumming appendages of ruffed grouse, silvery

blades of tern slicing the air from Arctic to
southern oceans, shivering sickle wings of swift
flying, sleeping, and making love in the heavens,
silent-as-snow pinions of owl, and emus and
ostriches who toss over the idea of flight
and do without.

Imagination embraces leaf-lobed toes of grebe,
branch-grasping phalanges of thrush, armored
talons of eagle, webbed paddles of duck,
bark-gripping, zygodactyly of woodpecker,
disemboweling daggers of cassowary, slender
splayed lily pad tiptoes of jacana, stalking stilts
of heron, and snowshoe-feathered feet of ptarmigan.
Meadowlarks and bustards stride through
grasslands on sturdy legs and feet, while swifts
need only tiny toes to cling to cliffs and
chimneys where they plaster their nests.

Feathers stream in diverse shapes and colors,
from emerald banner of resplendent quetzal,
to eponymous tail feathers of lyrebird,
feathered tiara of crowned crane, shape-shifting
spectacular bird-of-paradise, clock-pendulum
tail of motmot, coarse horsehair modified
feathers of kiwi, and water-repellant fish-scale
feathers of penguin. Colors shame
the rainbow spectrum—red-crested cardinal,
orange oriole, yellow-finch, green honeycreeper,
bluebird, indigo bunting, and violet-green swallow;

harlequin costumes beyond imagining—painted
bunting, paradise tanager, peafowl, rainbow lorikeet,
golden pheasant, mandarin duck, Gouldian finch.
But lest praise be limited to colors bright, we bow
to the beauty of brown and black—sparrow and
cisticola, grouse and seedsnipe, plover
and sandpiper, raven and drongo.

A multiplicity of avian religions,
personalities, and sexual strategies evolved
to fill the niches in our universe.
        Nightjars and oilbirds worship the night,
        sunbirds and vultures venerate the heat
        of the day, and solitaires sing psalms
        to the shadowy edges just before dawn.
The introvert in me loves the dipper, teetering
on his solitary rock in a remote mountain stream,
the tapaculo skulking in dark of thickest thicket,
but murres and terns peck out nest sites among
the hordes, exhibitionist sage-grouse and manakins
perform their dances under the critical eyes
of female judges, red knots and sandpipers party
on the beaches during migration, and
schools of starlings swim through the heavens
in magical murmurations.
        The love life of birds is an encyclopedia
        of options, most are monogamous, a few
        mate for life, others practice a serial version
        of love the bird you're with, although
        many step out on their mates when

they're not looking. Polygamists increase
their odds with crazy names for the game
of love, polygynous red-winged blackbird
male defends the reeds and a harem of females,
while polyandrous flashy female phalarope
mates with multiple males, leaving "house-
husbands" to tend nests, and
polygynandrous tinamous and Smith's
longspurs mix it all up in an orgy of
multiple males and females.
And the dream goes on and on—plover eggs
laid on the bare ground, kittiwake eggs teeter
on cliff faces, domed grasshopper sparrow nests
hidden beneath grass clumps, neatly woven
warbler cups in tree branches, pendulous
architecture of weaver and oriole, burrows
of kingfisher and barbet, huge stick
monstrosities of hamerkop, cavities of parrot
and woodpecker, while cuckoo and cowbird
drop eggs in some other hapless bird's nest,
and brush-turkey buries eggs
in heated compost heap and departs.

Let us revel in this amazing, magical,
evolutionary process of creation that has
brought forth avian legions and featherless,
wingless bipeds, through evolution and
extinction, over time and space. Share too,
the messages from my feathered dream.
It is a time, I think, to celebrate diversity,

mourn the loss of those we could have saved—
    great auk, passenger pigeon,
        Carolina parakeet, black mamo,
          ʻōʻō, Labrador duck, elephant bird,
        ivory-billed woodpecker, heath hen,
    dusky seaside sparrow,
unfist our souls finger by finger to release
the hope that perches there, ensure that nieces,
nephews, and grandchildren are not left
to eulogize fossils,
    faded photos, and
        dusty museum specimens.

Celebrate with me living feathered multitudes—
thirty-nine scientific orders, 237 families, and
over 10,000 living species, familiar names
and not so familiar—
rheas, megapodes, screamers,
    mesites, sandgrouse, potoos,
        cuckoos, turacos, hoatzins,
          thick-knees, plains-wanderers,
        skuas, sunbitterns, tropicbirds,
    loons, storks, boobies,
shoebills, secretarybirds,
    mousebirds, trogons, hoopoes,
        cuckoo-rollers, toucans, seriemas,
          caracaras, cotingas,
        whipbirds, crombecs,
    sugarbirds,
whydahs.

Oh, the variety, the differences,
among birds, among us,
that make us all
—together—
strong, beautiful, and extraordinary.

Learning to Fly

Last night
I met my mother
in a dream.
She has been gone
for more than a year.
        I do not know
where she has been.

All my willingness to
let the mystery be,*
flamed out when
someone I love walked
into the mist beyond
        what I know.

They say the dead
do not grow older;
she had instead
grown younger, shed
cancer's ashen brittleness.
Unlike anything
she did in life,
        she broke away

from me,
        sashayed down the path,
                swung her hips,
                        threw her arms wide
                like wings,
        sang, "See?
I feel fine!
        I've been
                learning
                        to fly!"

* lyrics by Iris DeMent

Glossary

acequia (Spanish): *irrigation ditch*

almendrado (Spanish): *made with almonds*

coloradito (Spanish): *a little red*

corvids: *birds in the family Corvidae, which includes ravens, crows, jays, and magpies*

cuidado (Spanish): *watch out, beware*

latilla (Spanish): *peeled branch or piece of wood laid between beams of a ceiling or above the vigas for decoration*

mole (Spanish): *a thick, cooked chile sauce*

negro (Spanish): *black*

ngoni (Mandingo and other African languages): *West African predecessor of the banjo; stringed instrument made of wood or calabash, with dried animal skin head stretched over it*

sipápu (Hopi): *a small hole in the floor of the kiva (an underground ceremonial chamber), representing the People's place of emergence from the preceding world*

Index of Illustrations

All pen-and-ink illustrations are by Janet M. Ruth. Unless otherwise noted below, photographs are also by Janet M. Ruth. The list is organized alphabetically by common name and page numbers are provided in parentheses.

ACKNOWLEDGMENTS

My husband, Dave Krueper, supported me in long months of field research and has been my partner on international birding/photography/writing adventures, from which so many of my poems and stories have been born. He listens to early drafts of my poems, comes to hear me read at open mics, and provides photos to inspire my drawings or accompany my writing. I am so thankful for his cassowary photo on the cover of this book. See his amazing photos on his Flickr site [https://www.flickr.com/photos/106773832@N02/]

The following poems and stories have been previously published or recognized.

"As If They Were Not There" in *Poets Speak Anthology* – *WALLS* – Vol. 4. 2018. Beatlick Press and Jules Poetry Playhouse Publications.
"Black Swifts" in *Weaving the Terrain: 100-Word Southwestern Poems.* 2017. Dos Gatos Press.
"Canticle to Change" in *Value: Essays, Stories & Poems by Women of a Certain Age.* 2017. Beatlick Press.
"crow can't get no satisfaction" in 2018 *Poets' Picnic.* Chapbook.
"Emergence" received First Honorable Mention in 2017 Alabama State Poetry Society Award Contest.

"Held Hostage by Trashers" in *Birding* magazine, March
2009.

"Living with Otus" in *Bird Watcher's Digest*, September/
October 2013.

"Owl Dreams" in *Grey Sparrow Journal/Snow Jewel*. Winter
2016.

"Swift Angels" in *Poets Speak Anthology – HERS – Vol. 2.*
2017. Beatlick Press and Jules Poetry Playhouse
Publications.

I thank Pattiann Rogers for permission to use an
excerpted stanza from "The Dream of the Marsh Wren:
Reciprocal Creation."

Standing before an audience of friendly faces to read my
poems out loud has increased my confidence. Thank
you to all the organizers of community poetry events in
the Albuquerque area where I have had the privilege of
reading. I am grateful to our wonderful regional presses
who have provided me with opportunities to publish
poems in anthologies—Beatlick Press, Jules Poetry
Playhouse Publications, and Dos Gatos Press. Sharing
poems, critiques, prompts, and rewrites with my Poetry
Prompt Group has improved my poems; thank you
Faith Kaltenbach, Scott Wiggerman, John Roche, Gayle
Lauradunn, Deb Coy, and Mikki Aronoff. Special thanks
go to my poetry kindred spirit—Andrea "Andi" Penner.
We have discovered, through sharing family stories,
that our mothers must have been long-lost sisters in a

previous life (collecting tea spoons and china tea cups, with violet patterns as a favorite!). Perhaps as a result of this crypto-cousinhood, we frequently find that we have written poems with similar themes and images. Thank you, Andi, for your friendship and encouragement in getting this book published.

I also want to acknowledge *The Feather Atlas* of the U.S. Fish & Wildlife Service Forensics Laboratory, where I found many of the reference photos for my pen-and-ink sketches of North American bird feathers. This resource can be found at [https://www.fws.gov/lab/featheratlas/].

Janet Ruth grew up in southeastern Pennsylvania, lived for almost 20 years in Washington, D.C. and Virginia, five years in Colorado, and has called Corrales, New Mexico home since 2001. As a child she enjoyed cross-country family camping trips, watching birdfeeders with her Mom, and going small game hunting with her Dad (she was the "dog"!). Much of her life has revolved around birds. This included her doctoral dissertation at George Mason University—"Effects of vegetation structure and surrounding land-uses on avian communities in the floodplain forests of Maryland"—and continued through field research with U.S. Geological Survey (USGS), resulting in scientific papers about winter grassland bird habitat preferences, songbird migration patterns in the US-Mexico borderlands using NEXRAD weather radar, and breeding ecology of Grasshopper Sparrows in southeastern Arizona and southwestern New Mexico. She has retired from a career as a research ornithologist although she continues to publish scientific manuscripts as an emeritus scientist.

Janet and her husband, Dave Krueper, have enjoyed international birding/photography/writing trips to Panama, Mexico, Belize, Peru, Brazil, Kenya, Tanzania, Madagascar, South Africa, and Australia. She writes daily journals during the trips and mines these volumes for poem and story ideas. In addition to the poems and stories in this book, she has published a story about their trip to the Atlantic rainforest of Brazil—"Brazil's Beautiful Mountain – Serra Bonita"—in *Birding* magazine.

Janet's poetry and stories are tightly bound to and inspired by her connections with the natural world. She often thinks of them as embodying all of the observations from the world around her that wouldn't fit into her scientific manuscripts. She is a member of the New Mexico State Poetry Society (NMSPS) and participates in the NMSPS Albuquerque Chapter, as well as multiple events in Albuquerque's active poetry community. She has had poems published in *Grey Sparrow Journal*, *Bird's Thumb*, *Santa Fe Literary Review*, *Duke City Fix*, and *The Ekphrastic Review*. She also has poems in regional anthologies including: *VALUE: Essays & Poems by Women of a Certain Age*; *A Poets Picnic: a Celebration of Nature, Calligraphy, Music & Poetry*; four volumes of *Poets Speak Anthology – HERS, WATER, WALLS,* and *SURVIVAL*; and *Weaving the Terrain: 100-Word Southwestern Poems*.

Made in the USA
Middletown, DE
19 February 2019